Solid Waste Management

About the Editors

Dr. Shyamli Singh is working as Assistant Professor with Indian Institute of Public Administration, New Delhi, India. She is the coordinator of the Centre for Environment and Climate Change. Dr. Singh has her Ph.D. in the ambit of Environmental Management. She has wide experience in research teaching and consultancy. She has published several research papers in international and national journals of repute. Dr. Singh has authored text books, monographs, articles and discussion papers. She is the lead Project Director of various prestigious projects and studies. She has more than ten years of working experience in different area of Environment. Dr. Singh is a Gold Medallist from Indraprastha University and a topper from University of Delhi.

Mr. Ashish Jain is a Post-graduate in Environmental Science and Founder Director of an NGO, Indian Pollution Control Association. He also holds position of Director in RecMech Enviro Pvt. Ltd., Avasa Technologies Pvt. Ltd., Air Quality Management Services, and Parshvi International. He has 15 years of professional experience in the field of Solid Waste Management and Environment Education and inventor of Aerosol Destruction Machine for the safe disposal of Aerosol Bottle and has patent for the Wall Mounted Baler. He has also developed manual and electric baler for the waste traders in rural areas.

Professor Vinod Kumar Sharma is currently Senior Professor, Disaster Management/Consultant at Indian Institute of Public Administration, and Executive Vice Chairman, Sikkim State Disaster Management Authority, Government of Sikkim.

He holds Ph.D. (Ecology and Environment) from Banaras Hindu University, Varanasi, India (1971) and P.G. Diploma in Resources Ecology, Banaras Hindu University, Varanasi, India (1970). He has held several positions that include: Chief of Party, Programme for Enhancement of Emergency Response (PEER), USAID funded programme for six Asian Countries; Coordinator National Centre for Disaster Management/Professor, Disaster Management at National Centre for Disaster Management. Prof. Sharma is a member of several committees that includes: High Powered Committee on Disaster Management Chaired by Shri J.C. Pant (1999-2001); Committee on Alakhnanda Floods (1998-1999); National Committee on Disaster Management Chaired by Mr. Sharad Panwar (2001-2003); Advisory Committee of State Disaster Management Authority, Government of Haryana (2010-Contd.); National Cyclone Mitigation Programme (National Disaster Management Authority, Govt. of India); Executive Vice Chairman, Sikkim State Disaster Management Authority, Government of Sikkim. A prolific writer, Dr. Sharma has 14 books and several other publications to his credit. His area of specialization includes environment and disaster management (Training and Research).

SOLID WASTE MANAGEMENT

Compendium of Case Studies

Shyamli Singh
Ashish Jain
Vinod K. Sharma

CONCEPT PUBLISHING COMPANY PVT. LTD.
NEW DELHI-110059

ISBN-13: 978-93-86682-74-1

First Published in 2019

Published and Printed by

Concept Since 1974

Concept Publishing Company Pvt. Ltd.
A/15-16, Commercial Block, Mohan Garden,
New Delhi-110059 (INDIA)
T : 91 11 25351460, 91 11 25351794
E : publishing@conceptpub.com; *W* : www.conceptpub.com

Cataloging in Publication Data--Courtesy: D.K. Agencies (P) Ltd. <docinfo@dkagencies.com>

Singh, Shyamli, author.
Solid waste management : compendium of case studies / Shyamli Singh, Ashish Jain, Vinod K. Sharma.
pages cm
Includes bibliographical references and index.
ISBN 9789386682741

1. Refuse and refuse disposal--India--Noida--Case studies. 2. Refuse and refuse disposal--India--Delhi--Case studies. I. Jain, Ashish, author. II. Sharma, Vinod K. (Vinod Kumar), author. III. Title.

LCC TD789.I52N65 2019 | DDC 363.7280954 23

Foreword

"Solid Waste Management: Compendium of Case Studies", which provides valuable insights into current practices in the cities and will serve as the key guiding tool for further implementation.

The compendium of case studies addresses sustainability of environment through solid waste management, awareness campaigns and trainings. This compendium highlights the lessons learnt at the course of duration and may be used as a resource for future initiatives moving towards the environmental sustainability.

This compendium provides a snapshot from initiatives undertaken, focusing on initiatives where valuable lessons could be drawn.

The compendium is designed to influence future progress by helping—to identify and disseminate case studies that provide examples of best practice. The review of case studies and initiatives is imperative as it brings out the best practices and loopholes, which can be plugged in with future learnings.

This is the first step in an ongoing collection of case studies and provides a selection of four episodes that are both illuminating and interesting. This selection is by no means exhaustive, definitive or exclusive. The authors wish to document many more case studies in the larger interest of the governance and community.

Prof. Suresh Misra
Professor of Consumer Affairs
Indian Institute of Public Administration
New Delhi

Preface

The book, "**Solid Waste Management: Compendium of Case Studies"** is motivated by the urgency of furthering the adoption of safe solid waste management practices in India. The management of solid waste is a national crisis. The number of available landfills is decreasing, the health risks associated with waste incineration are of great concern and the growing public / NIMBY opposition to sitting new waste management facilities is a growing problem especially for urban local authorities. There is need for policy intervention in an inclusive production-consumption-recovery pattern of waste management in India. The book tries to present a full picture of the state-of-the-art research and development of actionable knowledge discovery in new initiatives in solid waste management through a compendium of case studies. The inception of this compendium was triggered by applications of real-world challenges and complexities. Although there has already been a lot of documentation in this huge public services breakdown zone, there is no case study based approach on this burning issue. There seems to be a gap between academia and businesses and between academic research and ground realities in the context of popularizing waste management practices. This book is an attempt to address the ubiquitous challenges and complexities from a real-world perspective. It features practical progress in promoting initiatives. It presents recent developments and discoveries in solid waste management practice and its associated risks of air, water and soil pollution to stimulate more research and to rapidly pass on such discoveries to the community. The authors do intend to come up with such documentation in future too.

The intended clients would likely be researchers, research

students, policy makers, academia, practitioners, local community and decision makers. The book should also interest industry in working on sustainable development, solid waste management and related areas. It provides a coherent view of the state of the art and practice to enable developers and managers with technical and organizational approaches.

Acknowledgements

The success and final outcome of the studies required a lot of guidance and support from many people and organizations and we are extremely privileged to have got that. We would like to record our acknowledgements and thanks to those who have contributed in making this compendium as useful and purposeful as possible in its major objectives.

With an overwhelming sense of obligation, we avail this opportunity to express our deep sense of gratitude towards Mr. Pravin Mallick, Environment Director, Tetra Pak India Pvt. Ltd. and Ms. Neelima Khetan, General Manager, CSR, Coca Cola India Pvt. Ltd. who gave us the opportunity to work with the community to educate them on very important issue of source segregation.

We would like to take this opportunity to express its deep gratitude to PepsiCo India Holding Pvt. Ltd., Nestle India Ltd., Perfetti Van Melle India Private Ltd., Dharampal Satyapal Ltd., and Dabur India Ltd. for forming a consortium to implement India's first joint EPR. It is our privilege to express our profound indebtedness, to Dr. S.P. Singh Parihar (IAS), Chairman, CPCB, Dr. S.K. Nigam, Additional Director, CPCB, Dr. Ranbir Singh (IAS), Commissioner, EDMC; Mr. Pradeep Khandelwal, Chief Engineer, EDMC and Mr. Piar Singh, EE(SLF), EDMC, Delhi for their valuable guidance. We sincerely thank Shri Deepak Aggarwal, Sr. Vice President, IL&FS Environment for accepting our request to process collected MLP. Our special thanks to Mr. Ulhas Parlikar, Dy. Head, Geocycle India, ACC Ltd. and Mr. Sandeep Kapoor, Sales Head, Geocycle India, ACC Ltd. and for their kind co-operation and support to co-process MLP waste in their Cement Kiln Plants.

Thanks is also due to Mr. R.S. Yadav, Senior Project Engineer, Noida Authority; Mr. Pandey, Chandigarh Pollution Control

Board, Mr. Sandeep Garg, MD, ECO Group; Ms. Reena Chadha, Sr. Manager, EMS,ECO Group for their kind support and guidance.

We emphatically express our profound thanks and heartfelt gratitude to the Media Partner, Hindustan Times, waste collection partner Parkash Environmental Group, recycling partner Ganesha Ecoshpere Ltd. and Deluxe Recycling India Pvt. Ltd. and Knowledge Partner Global Communities India for their valuable guidance, timely suggestions and constant support and encouragement from preparation to execution of project.

We would like to thank Management Development Institute, Gurgaon and TERI University, New Delhi students from their contribution. We express our heartfelt thanks to M/s. DLF Estate Developers Ltd. and its staff, and Citizens Environmental Improvement Society (CEIS) for allowing and supporting us in execution of various awareness activities. This project was impossible to gain any momentum without the support from residents and their RWAs. Sincere thanks to RWAs of selected areas from Delhi and Noida city, DLF City RWA, Rich-Reg Condominium Association, Hamilton Court Condominium Association and their members.

Our sincere thanks the regional partners PACE, Sampurn(e)arth Environment Solution Pvt. Ltd. and Environment Matters for their co-operation and support in carrying out project activities in different cities.

The authors would fail in the acknowledgements if they do not thank Prof. Suresh Misra, Professor, IIPA who has always shown confidence and solidarity in authors.

Special thanks to Ms. Akanksha Singhal, Research Officer, IIPA for her untiring efforts. A big thank you to Concept Publishing Co. (P) Ltd., New Delhi for beholding trust in the authors.

Last, but not the least, the acknowledgements would be incomplete if we do not mention the hard work, support and co-operation shown by rag-pickers community and scrap dealers in achieving the targets within the timeline. The journey would have been impossible without them.

Finally, we thank all those who helped us directly and indirectly in implementation of projects.

New Delhi
Dated 19.09.2018

Shyamli Singh
Ashish Jain
Vinod K. Sharma

Introduction

Solid Waste Management: A Compendium is a collection of concise but comprehensive information. This Compendium comprises of four cases, which intend to serve the following purposes:

- The case studies can be incorporated into customized training materials to give them added relevance and realism.
- The studies can be used as 'reference points' or 'building blocks' to develop specific cases that reflect experience and issues of managing environmental components practice in a country or region of similar nature.
- To sensitize the readers and facilitate adoption of best practices as reflected in the case studies.

A selection of case studies, demonstrating solid waste management, environmental education, awareness and sensitization are included in the compendium. The deliverables are structured in the following case studies:

A brief summary of the case study is as given below:

Case I: **Knowledge, Attitudes and Practices on Household Solid Waste Management in Noida and Delhi city** is a survey by **IPCA**. The main problem of waste management in Noida and Delhi city is lack of waste management plan and lack of involvement of different stakeholders in systematizing waste collection and disposal. Therefore, this aims to assess the knowledge, attitudes and practices of residents towards solid waste management. It reflected that much work has to be done to create awareness and mobilize the communities to bring behavioural change in their practices towards the waste management. This survey can work as a baseline towards zero waste community. There is need for efforts from professional organizations such as health institutes, education sector, NGOs etc. who advocates for clean environment to work for promoting waste management education especially waste minimization and source segregation.

Case II: *Doh Bin*—Community participation has a direct bearing on efficient solid waste management. Yet, the municipal authorities have failed to mobilize the community and educate citizens on the rudiments of handling waste and proper practices of storing it in their own bins at the household, shop- and establishment-level. The mindset is primarily responsible for the unscientific systems of waste management in the country. ***Doh Bin*** an initiative, aims at sensitizing the masses and increasing their involvement to bring about a better waste management system in Gurugram (as the landfills around our city are filling up fast and this is leading to environmental problems) through the simple act of segregating wet and dry waste in our homes, offices etc., with the objective to maximum utilization of resources to reduce waste, which can indirectly result in less air, water and soil pollution, reduce pressure on landfill sites and reduce cost of transportation. It was initiated in DLF Phase-IV, Gurugram and created awareness through various programmes such as kid's carnival, senior citizens carnival, training of maids and waste collectors. The project has also set up dry waste collection centre to increase rate of recycling and promote hygienic and efficient waste management. The education and motivation of RWAs, residents, kids, domestic help and waste collectors to practice source segregation was initiated. It was seen that the initiative opened up avenues for volunteering to residents and professionals.

Case III: **We Care**, India's first Extended Producers

Responsibility (EPR) initiative—a pilot project executed proposed activities in eight metro cities (Delhi, Noida, Gurugram, Ghaziabad, Faridabad, Chandigarh, Mumbai and Dehradun) and companies to undertake implementation of their EPR obligation i.e., collection, segregation and recycling of the post consumed Multi Layered Packaging (MLP). To develop sustainable supply chain and strengthen segregation and collection of plastic waste, lot of serious efforts need to be done at the ground with the collaboration of various stakeholders. Keeping this in mind, IPCA has been engaged by the Consortium (PepsiCo India Holding Pvt. Ltd., Nestle India Ltd., Perfetti Van Melle India Private Ltd., Dharampal Satyapal Ltd., and Dabur India Ltd.) to deal on the issue and demonstrate their commitment to implement effective plastic waste management system in India. It aimed to educate and motivate waste collectors, set up dry waste collection centre, etc., and resulted in increased networking of the stakeholders and collected **683.115 MT** MLP and from which **663.115 MT** got processed.

Case IV: **Campaign for Pollution and its Remedial Measures** is an initiative to create awareness related to environmental pollution and its remedial measures among the school children. The project aimed to train and sensitize five hundred school children from ten schools (Amar Public School, Sector-37, Noida; Vivekanand International School; Lord Mahavira Model School, Sector-29, Noida; Laxmi Public School; Model National School, Sector-45 Noida; Marrigold Public School, Sector-19, Noida; Marrigold Public School, Greator Noida; Yash Memorial School; Sapphire International School; Arunodaya Public School) on various aspects of environmental pollution including identification of different kinds of pollution and its source, monitoring of pollutants, different approach to reduce its impact on individuals. The key objective of the campaign was to motivate students to come up with their own ideas to improve and conserve environment and implement their ideas in form of actions. Trends, challenges, solutions and lessons can be drawn from these case studies which may serve as a guide for the designing of initiatives in future. This compendium refers to lessons learnt as knowledge acquire from experiences. Collection is a mixed bag of positive or negative experiences, in both cases, they have led to insights, which benefit the development of future initiatives for better environmental management.

Contents

List of Tables and Figures

TABLES

FIGURES

Abbreviations

CEIS	Citizens of Environment Improvement Society
CPCB	Central Pollution Control Association
EPR	Extended Producer Responsibility
EWS	Economically Weaker Section
FDG	Focus Group Discussion
GDP	Gross Domestic Product
IPCA	Indian Pollution Control Association
KG	Kilo Gram
KOL	Key Opinion Leaders
MLP	Multi-Layered Packaging
MSW	Municipal Solid Waste
MSWM	Municipal Solid Waste Management
MT	Million Tonne
NGOs	Non-Governmental Organizations
PEG	Prakash Environmental Group
PWM	Plastic Waste Management
RWA	Resident Welfare Association
SWM	Solid Waste Management
TERI	The Energy and Resources Institute
TPD	Tonnes Per Day
WM	Waste Management

Case Study–I

Knowledge, Attitudes and Practices [KAP] Study on Household Solid Waste Management in Noida and Delhi City

A Knowledge, Attitude and Practices (KAP) survey is a quantitative method that provides access to quantitative and qualitative information. KAP surveys reveal misconceptions or misunderstandings that may represent obstacles to the activities that one would like to implement and potential barriers to behaviour change. Also, KAP survey essentially records an "opinion" and is based on the "declarative" (i.e., statements). Overall, it can—measure the extent of a known situation; provide new tangents of a situation's reality, enhance the knowledge, attitude, and practices of specific themes, establish the baseline, suggest an intervention strategy that are suited to the respective population involved (Monde, 2011).

1.1 Background

Whatever we consume generates a lot of garbage and waste. Discarding products adds to the clutter of the dustbins. But what happens with this garbage is a thought less pondered upon! The persistent increase in human population and rapid industrialization has caused the continuing global problems of improper wastes disposal. Cities worldwide are dying off under the aching load on them with tons of garbage and Indian cities are no better.

The major drawbacks concerning wastes management, especially in the developing countries are the ineffective waste collection strategies and the lack of disposal sites. It has been suggested, likewise, that the practices of basic Solid Waste Management (SWM) are often neglected at the individual level. While most people are aware of the negative environmental impacts of mismanaged wastes but their negative attitude coupled with insufficient environmental knowledge among individuals usually corresponds to poor practices towards maintaining good environmental conditions.

In Noida city, in the absence of a facility for solid waste disposal, the authority collects waste from primary garbage points (dump yards) and dumps the same randomly on a vacant land. Rag-pickers collect waste door to door and after picking out saleable items, dump the remaining garbage at nearby dump yards outside each residential area. This unregulated and unscientific system of garbage disposal causes pollution and health hazards for the public.

The various initiatives taken by Governmental, Non-Governmental Organizations (NGOs), private companies, and local public drastically increased in the past few decades. Nonetheless, landfills are still the dominant Solid Waste Management option for the Noida, Delhi and many other cities around the India. It is well known that waste management policies, as they exist now, are not sustainable in the long term. Thus, waste management is undergoing drastic change to offer more options that are more sustainable. We look at these options in the hope of offering the waste management industry a more economically viable and socially acceptable solution to our current waste management dilemma.

1.2 Problem Statement

Waste management is a major problem in India, especially in highly industrialized and densely populated cities like Delhi, Noida and the like. Noida, like many cities in India, suffers from improper Municipal Waste Management. Every day Delhi generates 9500 tonnes per day (TPD) of municipal solid waste and Noida 660 TPD, out of which 65 per cent is organic waste, 20 per cent is recyclable waste and the remaining 15 per cent is inert waste (waste such as chip packets, mud, construction debris). Due to unsystematic and improper waste collection and disposal, the whole city is gradually turning into a dump yard. The main problem of waste management in Noida and Delhi city is the lack of waste management plan and lack of involvement of different stakeholders in systematizing waste collection and disposal.

1.3 Purpose of the Study

The purpose of study is to assess the knowledge, attitudes and practices of residents in Noida and Delhi City towards the Solid Waste Management.

1.4 Objectives of the Study

- To assess the knowledge of residents on waste management.
- To assess the attitudes of residents towards waste management.
- To assess the practices of residents regarding waste management.

1.5 Study Area

The study area includes the three societies of Noida and two societies of Delhi City.

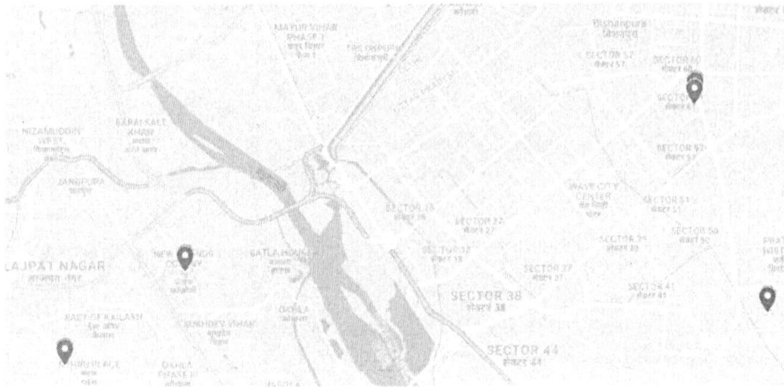

Figure 1.1: Locations of Study Areas

Table 1.1: Name of the selected societies and number of households

Sl. No.	*Name of Society*	*No. of Households*
1.	Sunshine Helios, Sector-78, Noida	240
2.	Saket Dham, Sector-61, Noida	122
3.	Indraprastha Villa, Sector-61, Noida	96
4.	New Friends Colony, South Delhi	300
5.	Delhi Govt. Officers Flats, Greater Kailash-1, Delhi	72

1.6 Methodology of Survey

The flow chart (Figure 1.2) depicts the methodology adopted for the study.

1.7 Data Collection Tools

The study used two kinds of data collection tools, one is questionnaire and another being the focus group discussion (FGD). Questionnaires were distributed among the residents of each society under the administration of researcher and Focus group discussion was also done to gather the information from the community leaders on the awareness and overall waste management system of the society.

1.7.1 Questionnaire

A questionnaire is a survey instrument used to collect data from individuals about themselves, or about a social unit such as a

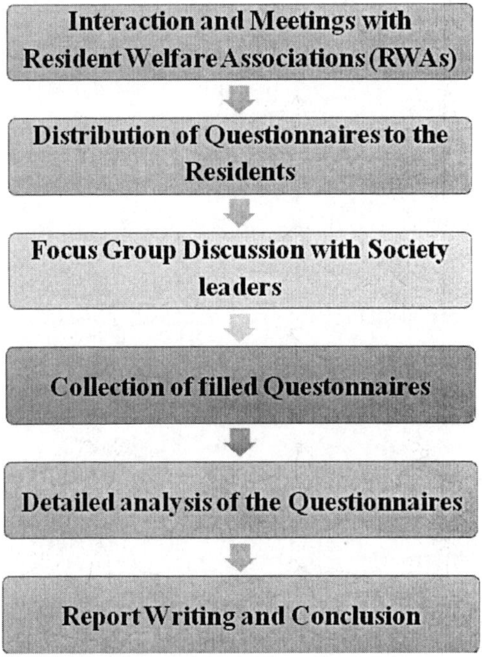

Figure 1.2: Steps of the Project

household or a school. The aim is to try to ensure that differences in responses to questions can be interpreted as reflecting differences among respondents (N. Ross, 2005). And as a research tool, two important concepts in questionnaire design: 'reliability' and 'validity' must be considered (Adams & Cox, 2008).

The questionnaires were distributed to all households of the society by RWA of the respective society. The residents were given sufficient time to fill the questionnaire and then the filled questionnaires were collected by RWA. This approach was adopted instead of going door to door and reading all the questions one by one by surveyors, because either all the respondents were not available due to their working hours or they were not willing to fill the form immediately. The questionnaire comprised of 22 questions [Annexure-I]. The questionnaire was used to collect all the basic information from a large population of all the societies. It provides 25.2 per cent retention of all the questionnaire and maximum utilization of the time. The questionnaire had both open ended and close ended questions. The open ended questions enabled the collection of information on knowledge, attitudes and practices of residents towards the waste management. These questions gave an opportunity to explore and clarify issues and collect qualitative data as well. The close ended questions helped to collect quantitative data on the identified issues.

1.7.2 Focus Group Discussion

Focus Group is a type of in-depth interview accomplished in a group, present characteristics defined with respect to the proposal, size, composition, and interview procedures. The focus or object of analysis is the interaction inside the group, in which a small group – usually 10 to 12 people – is led by a moderator (interviewer) in a loosely structured discussion of various topics of interest. It is a good way to gather together people from similar backgrounds or experiences to discuss a specific topic of interest. Further, these focus groups are used for generating information on collective views, and the meanings that lie behind those views. They are also useful in generating a rich understanding of participants' experiences and beliefs (Mishra, 2016).

In this study, the FGD was used to obtain information from the society leaders, especially information on waste management education such as source segregation, recycling and composting. The discussion was facilitated by the project coordinator and notes were taken. The advantage of this group discussion was that it allowed probing to obtain in-depth information.

1.8 Ethical Consideration

A letter of consent and project introduction was submitted to each RWA. This was done in recognition of their society and to gain their support and cooperation during the study. The project coordinator introduced himself/herself and the purpose was study was explained to them. No residents were forced to give information in case they are not willing to.

1.9 Challenges Faced in the Field

The study was not without the problems and difficulties. The coordinator had difficulties in mobilizing the community leaders for a focus group discussion, convincing them for the project activities and distribution of questionnaires. Due to negligence and negative attitude of people towards filling the questionnaire and giving it back, it took more than a week to collect the filled questionnaires from each society.

1.10 Presentation of Findings

1.10.1 Respondent's knowledge about Waste Management

The respondent's knowledge about solid waste management was assessed on the following criteria: knowledge of waste description and generation; danger of waste; knowledge about recycling of waste; knowledge about composting of waste; knowledge about sorting or separating and minimization of waste generation.

1.10.2 Overview of Respondent's Knowledge on Waste Management

The findings from the questionnaire reveal that the majority 91.86 per cent of respondents had not received any education about waste management. Only 8.13 per cent had received a form of education on waste management. Findings from the focus group discussion reveal that residents did not received any education or awareness on how to manage the waste.

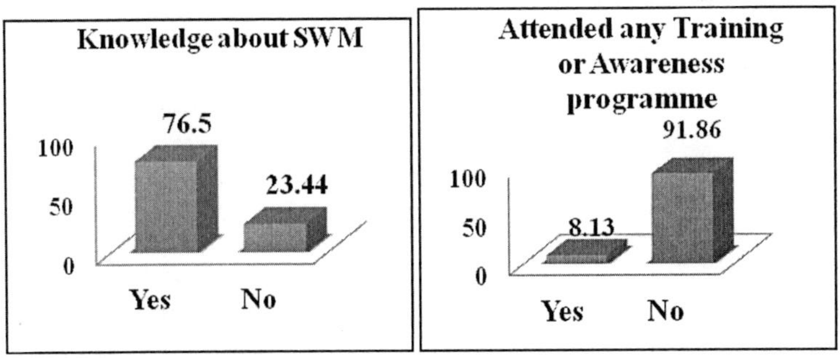

(a) (b)

Figure 1.3: (a) Respondent's having Knowledge about SWM (b)Respondents Attended any Training or Awareness Programme

1.10.3 Respondent's Knowledge: Source Segregation

Survey reveals that 42 per cent people are aware of source segregation but they do not know how to do source segregation, how should the waste be categorized.

1.10.4 Respondent's Knowledge: Wet and Dry Waste

Survey reveals that only 14 per cent people know about dry and wet waste. Unless they can differentiate between organic and inorganic waste, source segregation is not possible. So, there is need to educate people about dry and wet waste.

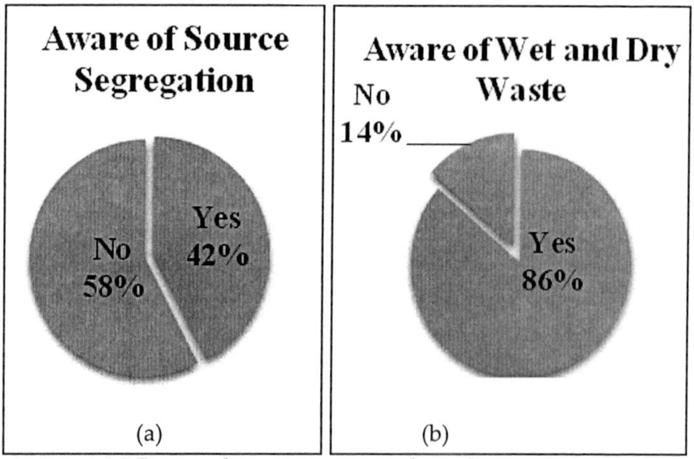

Figure 1.4: (a) Respondents Awareness about Source Segregation
(b) Respondents Awareness of Wet and Dry Waste Segregation

1.10.5 Respondent's knowledge about Recycling and Composting of Waste

A good percentage of residents are aware of recycling and composting but due to non- availability of any facility of recycling and composting they do not take any action to segregate their waste.

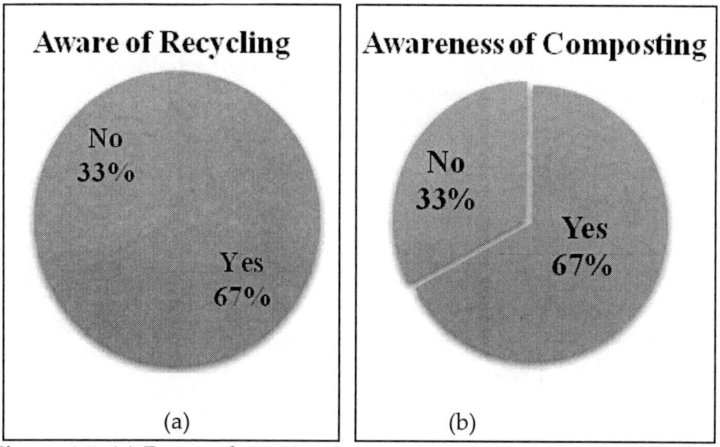

Figure 1.5: (a) Respondents Awareness about Recycling
(b) Respondents Awareness about Compositing

1.10.6 Respondent's Practice Regarding Waste Management

In this study, practice has been defined as participation in the management of the waste using different methods by the respondents. The assessment regarding practices included the aspects of: methods of waste disposal, minimization, recycling; composting, sorting or separating and waste collection.

1.10.7 Respondent's Waste Generation Rate and Type of Waste Generated

Residents in the selected societies discharge mix waste which contains largely food waste, paper, carton and plastic. The daily waste generation rate varies largely from 0.5 to 2 kg.

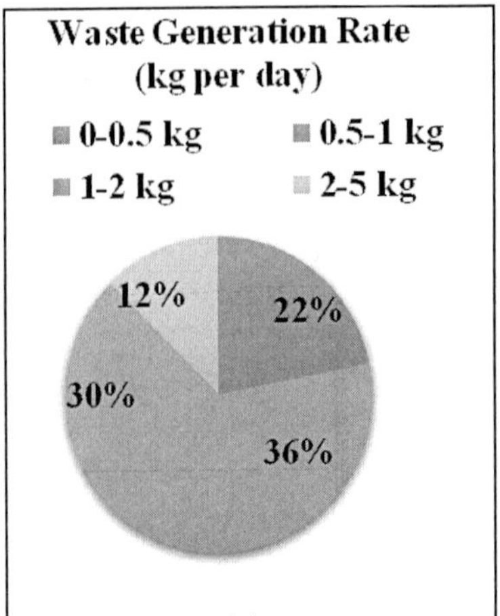

(a)

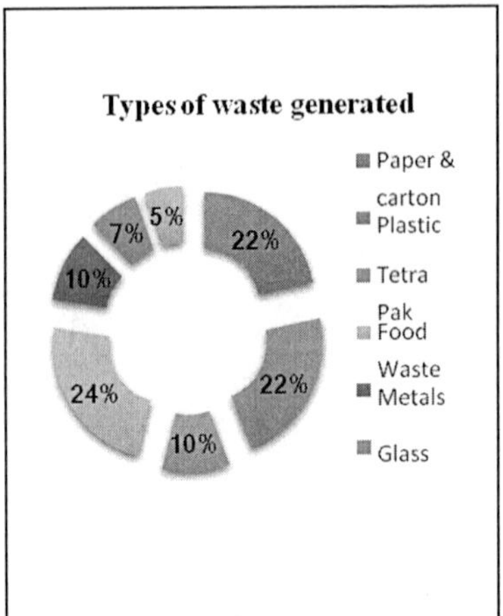

(b)

Figure 1.6: (a) Rate of Waste generation
(b) Types of Waste Generated

1.10.8 Number of Bins in the House

Majority of residents have only one bin in their house, which clearly reflects the poor condition of household waste management.

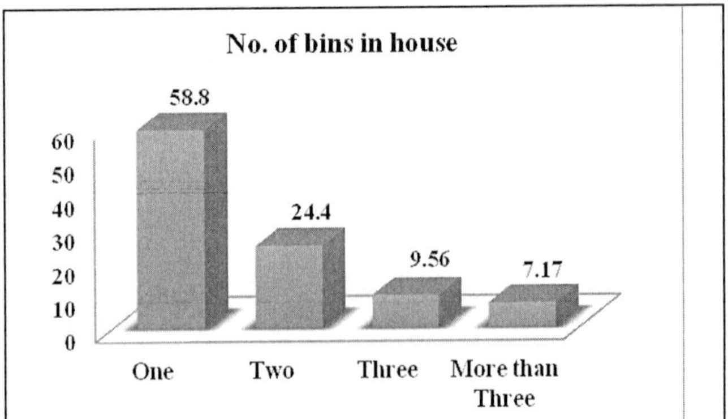

Figure 1.7: Number of Bins in Houses

1.10.9 Respondent's Method of Waste Disposal

Survey shows that in most of the societies informal door-to-door collection facility is available by informal sectors but still some residents dispose their waste in public bins or by other means, which shows poor waste management condition.

1.10.10 Practicing Source Segregation of Waste

Almost nobody is practicing source segregation. Some residents are doing so, but they do not follow the exact method of source segregation.

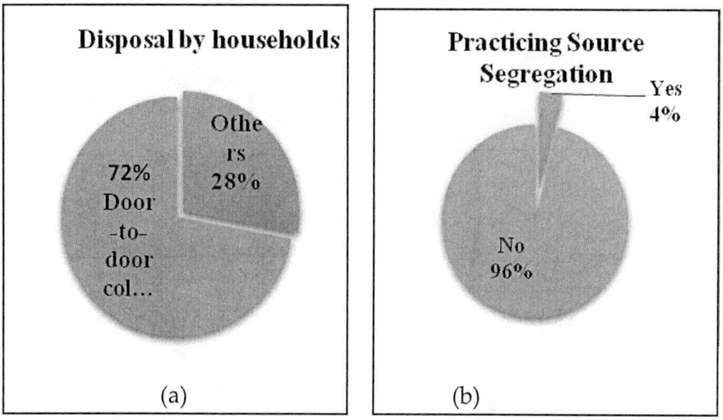

Figure 1.8: (a) Type of Waste Disposal by Households
(b) Respondents Practicing Source Segregation

1.10.11 Recycling and Composting of Waste

In societies, there are very few residents who are environmentally aware and give their waste to recycler for recycling. Study shows that nobody is practicing composting in societies but at their home town composting is in practice at some places.

1.10.12 Respondent's Satisfaction with Current Waste Management Service

Our study reveals that majority of residents are not satisfied with the waste management services in their area. They consider their area is not good for the health of residents as huge quantity of waste collected near their societies which decompose and results in stinking smell and unhygienic environmental conditions.

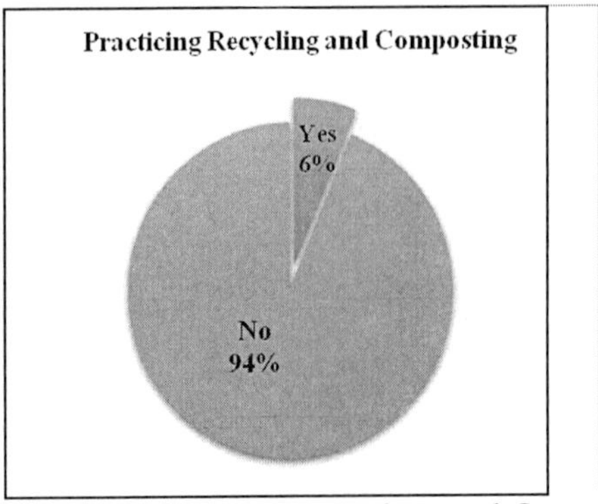

Figure 1.9: Respondents Practicing Recycling and Compositing

1.10.13 Attitude Towards Waste Management

Almost all the residents of the selected societies are willing to bring positive change in the environment. They want their society to be well maintained and hygienic and for that they are ready to extend any kind of support. They want to be educated and aware on household solid waste management and willing to do source segregation if proper guidance is available.

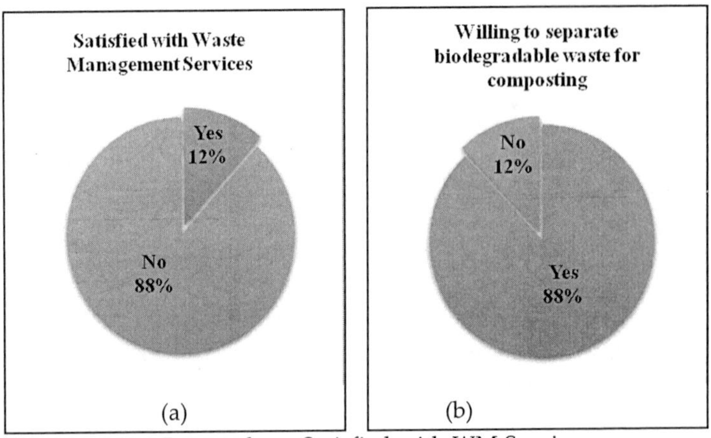

Figure 1.10: (a) Respondents Satisfied with WM Services
(b) Respondents Willing to Separate Biodegradable Waste for Compositing

1.10.14 Best Way to Communicate to them about SWM Practices

Residents of the societies are interested in being educated on solid waste management practices and most of the residents consider that the best way to communicate with them is organizing workshops in their societies and providing information on the community bulletin boards.

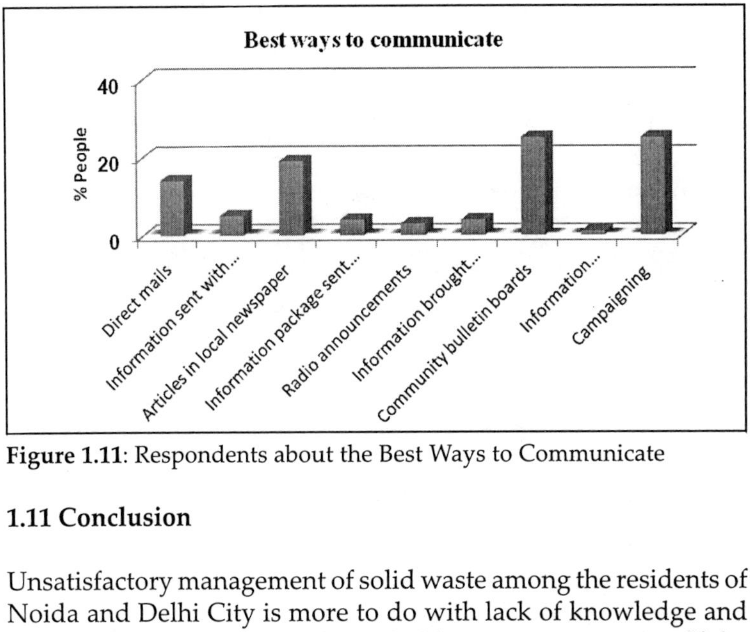

Figure 1.11: Respondents about the Best Ways to Communicate

1.11 Conclusion

Unsatisfactory management of solid waste among the residents of Noida and Delhi City is more to do with lack of knowledge and negative attitudes towards household waste management. If the residents can be empowered with knowledge which can be acquired through education and awareness their negative attitude will slacken. The practices are poor due to lack of education. Thus, much work has to be done to create awareness and mobilize the communities to bring behavioural changes in their practices towards waste management. There is need for efforts from professional organizations such as health institutes, education sector, NGOs and the like who advocates for clean environment to work for promoting waste management education especially waste minimization and source segregation.

ANNEXURE – I

Questionnaire on Household Solid Waste Management Practices

This survey is being conducted by Indian Pollution Control Association (IPCA) under the project "Awareness Campaign on Source Segregation and Home Composting" supported by Global Environment Management. Under this project we will install AEROBINS (Waste Composting Bins) in your society and will also organize awareness campaigns on source segregation and on proper waste management practices. The purpose of this quantitative and qualitative survey is to assess Knowledge, Attitude and Practices of the local people towards the Solid Waste Management. Based on your responses we will install Aerobins and organize awareness campaign in your society. We would appreciate you taking time to complete the survey.

Name: ____

Sex: ☐ Female ☐ Male Age: ________________

Address: ____

Phone No.: ____

No. of people in household: Adults ______ Children _______

Occupation: _______________________________________

Questions on Waste Management Practices

1. Do you know about Solid Waste Management?
   (i) Yes ☐ (ii) No ☐
2. Have you ever been educated or attended any training or awareness programme on waste management by any NGO/ULB/Municipality?
   (i) Yes ☐ (ii) No ☐
3. What type of solid waste is being generated by you and your family? (One or more option)
   - o Paper and carton
   - o Plastic (carry bag/PET bottles/MLP/LDPE/HDPE)
   - o Tetra Pak
   - o Food waste (left over/fruits and veg peels)
   - o Tins/cans/metals

- o Glass
- o Electronic waste (ink cartridge/CDs/DVDs/old TVs/ electric cords)
- o Others

4. How much waste do you generate per day?
   (i) 0-0.5 kg (iii) 0.5-1 kg (v) No idea
   (ii) 1- 2Kg (iv) 2-5 kg
5. How many bins do you have for storage of waste?
   (i) One (iii) Two
   (ii) Three (iv) More than three
6. Do you do source segregation?
   (i) Yes (ii) No
   If YES, How?________________________________
   If NO, Why?________________________________
7. Are you aware of wet and dry waste?
   (i) Yes (ii) No
8. How do you dispose your waste?
   - o In the public bin
   - o on road/ street side
   - o On any open space
   - o Door-to-door collection by authorities/private
   - o Others
9. If door-to door collection facility is available, then what is the mode of collection and transportation?
   - o Hand cart
   - o Tricycle
   - o TATA Ace
   - o Compactor
   - o Others

10. Do you know where waste collector disposes off the waste that he collects from your house?
   (i) Yes (ii) No
   If YES, then mention the place if known______________
11. Is your waste collector segregating waste materials?
   (i) Yes (ii) No
12. Do you think the method used by waste collectors for waste collection, segregation and disposal safe for waste collectors and environment?
   (i) Yes (ii) No

If No, any suggestion______________________________

13. Do you practice composting?
    (i) Yes (ii) No
    If YES, How much (organic) waste is used for composting?
    (i) 0–0.5 kg (iii) 0.5–1 kg (v) No idea
    (ii) 1– 2Kg (iv) 2–5 kg
14. If composting facility is available in your society, would you be willing to separate your bio-degradable waste for composting purpose?
    (i) Yes (ii) No (iii) Not Sure
15. Are you aware of waste recycling?
    (i) Yes (ii) No (iii) Not Sure
    If YES, then according to you what kind of waste can be recycled?______________________________
16. Are you satisfied with waste management services in your area?
    (i) Yes (ii) No (iii) Don't know
17. What is the best way to communicate to you about waste management programmes?
    - o Direct mails
    - o Information sent with utility bills
    - o Articles in local newspaper
    - o Information package sent once or twice per year
    - o Radio announcements
    - o Information brought home by school children
    - o Community bulletin boards
    - o Information Town/Country Web Sites
    - o Campaigning and public education programmes
    - o If any other, Kindly mention_______________
18. What problems do you think exist in your area as for waste management?

    ____

    ____
19. In your opinion, how can the problems of solid waste management can be resolved?

    ____

    ____

Thanks for taking out time for helping us keep _____________ (Society Name) clean and green.

HAPPY COMPOSTING

Case Study–II

"Doh Bin"

IPCA incorporated as Non-Governmental Organization (NGO) in 2001 and since then it is working with the rag-picker community and executing projects on Solid Waste Management and meanwhile IPCA has also experienced in disseminating environmental education. IPCA is running two projects under the aegis of Department of Environment, Government of Delhi, NCT on environmental education for Eco-Club in Schools of Delhi. IPCA has conceived two projects "Garbyhog-Home Builders Project" and "Tenderella and her herb Aid Box" for schools to disseminate knowledge on vermicomposting and medicinal plants and already worked with more than 200 schools in last five years and educated 10,000 students on vermicomposting technology and uses of traditional medicinal plants through fun learning activities.

IPCA provides services of waste collection, segregation, recycling and disposal for different sectors of our society including residential, corporate, institutes and industries and form a team of rag-pickers to execute these services. Approximately 700 Rag-picker from Delhi, Noida and Gurugram are associated with Indian Pollution Control Association for waste management projects. These rag-pickers are migrants from West Bengal, Assam, Eastern Uttar Pradesh, and Bihar and earning their livelihood by collecting waste material from different sources.

2.1 Background

Solid waste management is one amongst the basic essential services provided by municipal authorities in the country to keep urban centres clean. However, it is one of the most poorly rendered services in the basket—the systems applied are unscientific, outdated and inefficient; population coverage is low; and the poor are marginalized. Waste is littered all over leading to unsanitary living conditions. Municipal laws governing the urban local bodies do not have adequate provisions to deal effectively with the ever growing problem of solid waste management. With rapid urbanization, the situation is becoming critical. The urban population has grown fivefold in the last six decades with 285.35 million people living in urban areas as per the 2001 Census and the per capita waste generation ranges between 0.2 kg and 0.6 kg per day in the Indian cities amounting to about 1.15 lakh MT of waste per day and 42 million MT annually. Also, as the city expands, average per capita waste generation increases.

Community participation has a direct bearing on efficient SWM. Yet, the municipal authorities have failed to mobilize the community and educate citizens on the rudiments of handling waste and proper practices of storing it in their own bins at the household-, shop- and establishment-level. For the general public, which is quite indifferent towards garbage disposal etiquette, the onus of keeping the city clean is entirely on the ULBs. This mind set is primarily responsible for the unscientific systems of waste management in the country.

Besides economic benefits of improving the current waste management process in India, there are also a number of environmental benefits associated with an improved process. Under the current waste management process, the formal (government-run) sector can only handle about 30 per cent of the waste produced. This means that the majority of the remaining waste is handled by the informal sector. The informal/unorganized sector does not have the knowledge and capability to efficiently recover the material, and this subsequently leads to a low recycling rate of around 10-14 per cent (Zia, Devadas, & Shukla, 2008, p. 600). The formal sector's inability to handle the waste produced and the informal sector's low recycling rate lead to waste accumulating in informal dumpsites or on the streets. Finally, there are also a number of important social benefits to an improved waste management process. The current waste management process results in low self-esteem among rag-pickers. Rag-pickers are also faced with many health issues stemming from the lack of preventive measures taken while collecting waste (improper clothing, lack of protective clothing), the number of diseases harboured within the piles of accumulated waste, and the inability to access the government healthcare network or afford private healthcare. Most of the rag-pickers are illiterate, and as children often work with their parents, they do not have the ability to attend school.

IPCA believes that environmental issues are fundamental to the future health and well-being of our planet. Thus, we seek to understand the impacts of our activities on the environment at local, regional and global levels and we should work together to minimize these impacts. With this mindset, IPCA executed the project *Doh Bin* with the support of all stakeholders.

2.2 Project Description

Doh Bin is a pilot project aimed at sensitizing the masses and increasing their involvement to bring about a better waste management system in Gurugram through the simple act of segregating wet and dry waste in our homes, offices etc. The landfills around our city are filling up fast and this is leading to environmental problems. By segregating wet and dry waste, we will not just control what is being sent to the landfills but also improve the use of our limited resources through recycling. Source segregation leads to the collection of clean recyclables by waste collectors. This in turn, not only increases recycling, but also improves their income and livelihoods.

The project was initiated in DLF Phase-IV, Gurugram. *Doh Bin* created awareness through various programmes such as kid's carnival, senior citizens carnival, training of domestic help and waste collectors. The project has also set up dry waste collection centre to increase rate of recycling and promote hygienic and efficient waste management. The project has educated and motivated RWAs, residents, kids, domestic help and waste collectors to practice source segregation. The project has also given volunteering opportunities to residents and professionals.

2.3 Objectives

The prime objective of the project was to maximize utilization of resources to reduce waste, which can indirectly result in less air, water and soil pollution, reduce pressure on landfill sites and reduce cost on transportation. Project was also designed to increase per capita income of Rag-Pickers and their good health through following objectives:

(i) To increase the per capita income of waste collectors and contractors.
(ii) To reduce the cost on storage and transportation through compact baling of waste material.
(iii) To provide safe and hygienic environment to the waste collectors
(iv) To increase the recycling rate of Municipal solid waste through efficient segregation.
(v) To stop the illegal use and recycling of waste material through monitoring and introduction of authorized recyclers to the facility.
(vi) To eliminate the role of supplier and middle man in the Municipal Solid Waste (MSW) Supply Chain.
(vii) To get segregated waste at source.
(viii) To educate waste generators/consumers on efficient waste management.
(ix) To promote local self-responsibility for a clean environment.

IPCA also tried to work on an improved waste management process and propagation model in terms of the design of the collection system, analysis of current trends, set up of dry waste collection centre, improving operations at dry waste collection centre.

2.4 Project Area (DLF Phase-IV, Gurugram)

The project area is spread in 246.56 acre area, which is divided into plotted area with 1296 dwellings of high income group population with and 330 dwellings of Economically Weaker Section (EWS) and six multi-story residential complexes (*Ridgewood Estate, Hamilton, Windsor, Regency Park-I, Regency Park-II,* and *Regency park*). Project area also has four market complexes (*Galleria, Super Mart-I, Super Mart-II,* and *Cross Point*), one city club, and one Senior Secondary School (*Sri Ram Public School*).

In the identified project area, informal sector (*rag-pickers* and *kabadiwala*) plays a critical role in waste management and exist as a parallel system to the formal waste management process.

Following were the observations of project area before the execution of project:

- Plotted area served by an NGO "Parkash Environmental Group" for the door-to-door collection of household garbage.
- Five Waste collectors from PEG used to collect mixed garbage which was carried on a big bag and was kept on tricycle.
- There was no source segregation of household waste and there was no infrastructure and mechanism to encourage residents to segregate their waste.
- DLF Estate Developers Ltd. provided small piece of land to PEG for primary segregation in the green belt of DLF Phase-I.
- Multi-storey apartment served by facility management agency for all civic amenities and household waste was being collected by housekeeping staff from each household in single bin, which was later dumped at common point or garbage room of that apartment.
- Each apartment has its own waste management agency (waste contractor) and the agency took away all the

garbage at its centre by its own transport system (tractor trolley or tricycle).

- Segregation has been practiced by this informal sector at different places in a very unhealthy and unhygienic manner and quantity of waste recovery after segregation varies within the informal sector.

2.5 Launch of Project

Municipal solid waste is being generated by everyone and Municipal Corporation is the pioneer authority to manage it. During the execution of the project, we observed that Municipal Solid Waste in Gurugram was being managed by waste management agencies with the help of informal sector of rag-pickers and there was lack of awareness on ill impact of inefficient waste management and lack of knowledge on recycling applications of waste among the people. It was found that waste management was just not about generator and collector, it was also about Municipal Corporation, NGO, Recyclers, Corporate, Activist, Media etc. and it was decided to bring all these stakeholders to a common platform and launched *"Doh Bin"* in partnership with all major stakeholders.

Project Team launched the Project *"Doh Bin"* on 1st December, 2013 at Galleria Market, DLF Phase IV with joint efforts from Tetra Pak India Pvt. Ltd., Coca Cola India Pvt. Ltd. and Hindustan Times. Project was also supported by Parkash Environmental Group, DLF City RWA, Ganesha Ecoshpere Ltd., Deluxe Recycling India Pvt. Ltd., Global Communities India, Municipal Corporation of Gurugram and the residents of project area.

Joint Commissioner, MCG was invited as Chief Guest to launch the project logo, who was joined by the Vice President – Corporate Affairs, Coca Cola India Pvt. Ltd., Managing Director, Tetra Pak India Pvt. Ltd., General Secretary, DLF City RWA, and Director, IPCA. All these dignitaries flagged off to two chambers Cart.

Students from St. Mary School, New Delhi also joined the launch event and performed street play with message of environment conservation and protection. Their performance appealed the residents and left intense impression on the community.

Project team has also invited professional artists who made the event ambience more vivacious. They tried to educate people through fun and entertainment. e.g. people from gathering were invited on the stage and asked to participate in rapid fire session. Professionals also performed street play with a message of source segregation.

2.6 Methodology

The project addressed the problem of source segregation of municipal solid waste and its management. It also aimed to increase public awareness on economic, social and environmental aspects of the waste management. The project involved working in close collaboration with the resident welfare association, civic authorities, and taking advocacy initiatives to work with local residents to improve the general level of sanitation and cleanliness.

Project started with re-design of waste collection rickshaw into two compartments for the collection and transportation of segregated waste (dry and wet). Local residents, waste collectors, waste management agencies, print media (Hindustan Times) has played an important role in the project and shown ownership to the project, which was the basic need of the project for its grand success. Each stakeholder was made aware of the disastrous situation with regard to solid waste management and health. To achieve the above-mentioned objectives the project team has adopted two approaches:

1. **Awareness and Education:** Under this section, project team has organized various events and activities with the objective to exchange information on waste management and encourage residents to segregate their waste at source.
2. **Infrastructure for efficient Waste Management:** Under this section, project team has worked on designing and fabricating of two chamber cart, set up of dry waste collection centre and worked on tools to increase recycling rate and per capita income of waste collectors.

2.6.1 *Awareness and Education*

2.6.1.1 Development of education material: Project was initiated with the efforts to develop education material like logo, pamphlets, posters and other communication material. Since, the project aimed to bring behaviour change in the society towards waste management, it was very important to design and develop right education material for right people with right information. The developed educational material is demonstrated in Exhibit 2.1.

2.6.1.2 Door-to-door campaign: After the successful launch of the project, it was the time to interact with people and to sensitize them about *Doh Bin's* initiative and requested the masses to support the initiative by segregating their waste into two categories (Dry and Wet).

Project team used different tools for door-to-door campaign, which are as follows:

- **(i) Volunteers:** Eight students from Management Development Institute, Gurugram joined the initiative for volunteering and did door-to-door campaign on every weekend. They covered almost every household of plotted area and brainstormed about the need of source segregation and told them that by putting a little extra effort a lot of change can be brought in the society. They also distributed pamphlets and kits with two colour garbage bags (sponsored by DLF City RWA).
- **(ii) Waste collector:** Project team imparted training to the waste collectors and used him as the ambassador of the project campaign. He was the only person, who interacted with each family of project area every day. Therefore, he was the best person to spread the message for source segregation. During his door-to-door collection of garbage, he also asked residents to handover segregated waste.

(iii) Field staff: IPCA, the implementing agency of *Doh Bin* has also appointed field staff for day to day liaisoning with the residents and RWAs.

2.6.1.3 Training of domestic helpers: Since the project area was dominated by the population of high income group people, who have part time or full time domestic helpers at their home for domestic work like cleaning, dusting, washing, cooking etc. therefore, they played a key role in segregating waste at household level and project team decided to organize training session for domestic helpers on every 10th day of each month. But it was very difficult to have all domestic helpers at one time; therefore, project team had to organize number of session on schedule date. The activity was very much supported by the residents as domestic helpers were taught on segregation practices and categories of waste into bio-degradable and recyclable. They were also made aware about the benefits of waste segregation on environment. To encourage and motivate them for source segregation initiative, project team also distributed refreshment packets to the domestic helpers in the training session.

2.6.1.4 Training of waste collectors: Waste collectors visited residents of project area every day for the collection of household garbage. Therefore, it was very necessary to educate and train them on source segregation so that they could communicate the right message to the residents. Training of waste collectors was also very crucial so as to increase their per capita income. Project team also educated them on different waste categories, which needs to be recycled and has good economic returns. They were also sensitized about the available buyers and recyclers for different waste commodities.

2.6.1.5 Brainstorming session with volunteers: First Saturday of every month was scheduled for brainstorming session with volunteers. These sessions were very helpful to understand the need and problems of residents and helped the project team to develop future action plan. Several creative ideas developed during such sessions.

2.6.1.6 Kid's carnival: Kids are a very special part of our society and very useful platform to bring behavioural change in society. They are very useful medium to disseminate message in their family, friends, neighbour etc. and to use this power of society, project team decided to develop fun game and educate kids of project area through fun game. Project team organized numbers of kid's carnival at different locations with the objective to sensitize the young minds about managing their own waste and asked them to take this learning to their home, school, and neighbours. Kid's carnival was also experimented with activities like "*Click* and *Win Completion, Recycling Art, Quiz Show* and *Street Plays*" on waste segregation and won recycled note books as token prize.

2.6.1.7 Senior's Citizen Carnival: Project area was also very dominated by large population of senior citizens. These people had rich experience of life and could be a potential resource in bringing behavioural change among the people for source segregation of waste. Therefore, the project team organized Senior's Citizen Carnival in the project area and encouraged them to join the carnival. The project team invited experts from health and waste management in the carnival. The Health experts discussed on their health issues and gave them very useful tips for healthy life on the other hand waste management experts discussed on the benefits of source segregation on social, economic, and environment aspects and urged them to join the campaign by starting segregation of the waste at their home and also asked others to follow. The event was attended by large number of people and was very much appreciated.

2.6.1.8 Exhibition of recycled products: Since the project aimed to educate people on efficient waste management practices, which also included educating them on recycling applications of waste materials. Therefore, project team displayed recycled products from used tetra Pak cartons and PET bottles. People were amazed to see those products and this activity helped people to understand the direct impact or benefit of their little efforts during disposal of waste into dustbin. Many people who visited the exhibition stall at project area pledged to start segregation of waste and ask others too to follow.

2.6.1.9 Street play: To keep the momentum alive and spread the message to masses, project team used the tool of street play. Professionals performed plays on weekends at project area and attracted large number of people. People got entertained and received message of "why to segregate waste".

2.6.1.10 Study on municipal solid waste management: Understanding the ground reality: Three students from The Energy and Resources Institute (TERI) University joined the project for their partial fulfillment of Degree in Master of Science in Environmental Studies and Resource Management as interns and they carried out study on "Municipal Solid Waste Management: Understanding the Ground Reality" in Richmond Park, DLF Phase-IV. They carried out the study with the following objectives:

- To assess the composition of solid waste generated in the project area.
- To assess the amount of wet and dry waste generated by each household, daily.
- To assess if the present model of the project, *'Doh Bin'* is replicable to other condominiums or not.
- To analyse the entire supply chain of municipal solid waste management and understand the ground realities.
- To critically analyse the roles and responsibilities of every actor in Municipal Solid Waste Management (MSWM), and then suggest fruitful measures to improve the management of waste in India.

Students were also involved in creating awareness and training of domestic helpers and they helped to achieve segregation rate upto 50 per cent at Richmond Park.

2.6.1.11 Environment day celebration: Project team celebrated World Environment Day on 5th June, 2014 with kids and residents of Richmond Park. Project team talked about air, water, soil pollution, climate change with main emphasis on source segregation and efficient waste management. The team also organized environment quiz competition and games for kids and distributed recycled gift hampers.

2.6.1.12 Facebook page and website: Team used social media, which is very popular among the young generation and updated all event and activities on facebook. *Doh Bin* facebook page (www.facebook.com/dohbin) was liked by 408 people from different locations and professions. Project team also shared valuable information, video and pictures on waste management through facebook page. Project team has developed website for project *Doh Bin* (www.doh-bin.com) and tried to educate people thru webpage also. *Doh bin* webpage has been updated with information on dry and wet waste categories and why is important to segregate waste.

2.6.1.13 Print media: The media partner Hindustan Times played a very crucial role in highlighting the *Doh Bin* and waste management issue in Gurugram. Hindustan Times published pre- and post-event coverage along with interviews of stakeholders including residents, experts, Municipal Corporation and brought the issue of waste management in Gurugram in the mainstream. Now, *Doh Bin* is not restricted to project area boundary, it is being discuss in other residential complexes, meetings, and workshops. Media has also published factoids on waste recycling as an information tool.

Newspaper Clips on *Doh Bin*

2.6.2 *Infrastructure for Efficient Waste Management*

Exhibit 2.2: Two Chambered Cart

2.6.2.1 Introduction of the two chambered cart: During the project execution, it was observed that the waste being collected and transported in mixed form in one big bag. This practice might discourage or de-motivate the residents, who intended to do source segregation of waste. Therefore, it was decided to launch a two chamber cart. The two chambered cart were plied by waste collectors in project area and were appreciated by the residents. Two chambered carts have helped the project team to initiate the talks on source segregation and waste management and start the momentum of source segregation practices. Exhibit 2.2 displays two chambered cart launched by IPCA.

2.6.2.2 Set up of dry waste collection centre: *Doh Bin* was not about just creating awareness and educating people, it was also about creating adequate infrastructure required for efficient waste management. IPCA and its waste collection partner Parkash Environmental Group has worked together to set up a Dry Waste Collection Centre as shown in Exhibit 2.3 at Village Ghitorni, New Delhi. Centre was set up with the following objectives:

(i) Provide all necessary infrastructure like fire extinguisher, safety, water, electricity, hydraulic baler, rest room etc.
(ii) Different section for different waste commodities.
(iii) Provide regular training to the waste contractors and waste collectors to segregate waste in more efficient manner.

(iv) Channelize segregated waste to authorized and legal recyclers.
(v) Increase per capita income of waste collector.

To meet above mentioned objectives, project team made sections in the centre for different waste commodities and provided regular training to the workers on segregation and storage of waste material. They were also provided with gloves and mask for their better health and asked them to wear them during their work hours.

To reduce workload on the workers and to save cost on storage and transportation, IPCA installed Vertical Hydraulic Baler at the centre and provided training to the workers on the working of the Baler.

Project team also worked to increase per capita income of waste collectors and linked waste collectors to the recyclers and they received more value to their waste material.

Exhibit 2.3: Dry Waste Collection Centre

2.6.2.3 Door-to-door collection of household waste: Collection partner Parkash Environmental Group (PEG) has supported the project by providing its team of waste collectors for the collection of municipal solid waste from plotted area and Richmond Park. PEG has also supported in collection of segregated municipal solid waste in two separate bags.

2.6.2.4 Composting: Project team helped Rich-Reg Condominium Association for composting horticulture waste. Project team dug two pits in the backyard of Richmond Park and trained their horticulture staff to put all the tree and grass cutting into the pit. Project team has also provided them Effective Microorganism Solution to accelerate the decomposition rate.

Exhibit 2.4: Installed bin for e-waste

Install bins for E-waste: The residents of Richmond Park wanted to extend their segregation practices to next level by segregating e-waste and they asked project team to link them with e-waste recycler and recycled bins for the storage of e-waste separately. To encourage this intention, project team has installed four bins as shown in Exhibit 2.4 at Richmond Park Compound for separate storage of e-waste and channelized their e-waste with the e-waste recycler.

2.7 Result and Discussion

Doh Bin was executed at DLF Phase-IV, Gurugram and there is an approximate total of 280 flats within the complex. Richmond Park is a high class condominium with financially sound inhabitants.

The status of the complex was also reflected in the type of waste generated by the residents. Waste characterization is a key factor that is to be studied before making any solid waste management plan, as the type of waste generated varies with a change in the income of waste generator.

- Total training for Maids and servants: 14
- Total Participants: 173
- Total Trainings for Waste collectors and Housekeeping Staff: 11

Table 2.1: Number of total dwellings in each selected area, and the number of residents practicing segregation of waste

	Total No. of Dwellings	*Segregate*	*Do not segregate*	*No response*
Richmond Park	280	172	108	0
Hamilton Court	266	205	61	0
Garden Villa	35	17	18	0
Chander Lok	200	110	90	0
Plotted Area (surveyed by Chic)	714	303	206	204

- Total Participants: 126
- Total Training of residents: 3
- Total Participants: 52
- Total Carnivals: 7
- Total Participants: 277
- Total Exhibition: 3

2.7.1 Challenges

Following are the challenges faced during the implementation of the project:

- Most of the maids and the servants give their services to multiple households. Their time is fixed with every house and it is back to back. Therefore, even after repeated announcements it was very difficult to convince the maids and the servants to attend the training programmes.
- Residents showed apathy towards the project. They were not sparing much time to listen nor were they attending the training sessions regularly.
- The policy of the project was that the residents had to buy the bins and IPCA will not provide the bins and garbage bags. It became one of the biggest challenges to convince the residents that they have to buy the bins and the garbage bags.
- The rag-pickers segregated the waste by naked hands. After repeated training and providing the safety equipment like gloves, shoes and masks they did not use them.
- RWAs did not participate actively in the promotion of *Doh Bin*. They were only giving the permission to implement the project.
- Residents were reluctant to meet the implementing agency.

2.7.2 Learning

- Proper plan/guidelines and strategy should be in place before starting the implementation of the project.
- Role of the funding agency and the implementing agency should be clearly stated.
- To increase the participation of maximum citizens, we should organize common carnivals instead of specific carnivals like Kids and Senior citizen carnival.
- The awareness campaign needs to be more rigorous and innovative.

2.7.3 Recommendation

- Instead of big events once in two months there should be multiple events in every RWA especially in the plotted areas.
- Training modules for waste collectors, residents and maids and servants should be developed and field tested and trainings should be followed as per the manual.
- RWA should pass some kind of resolution stating (example) (1) those who do segregation will be acknowledged; (2) those who do not will be fined; (3) RWA will not pick up the garbage if people don't segregate.
- This project should be participatory (the residents should be also made accountable).

2.7.4 Conclusion

- The target has been achieved by the funding agency for the project.
- Leads to increase the income and improve health of Rag-pickers.
- There is decrease in the waste going to landfills.

2.8 Achievements

The biggest achievements of the project are discussed as under:

1. Project was successfully executed at plotted area of DLF Phase-IV and Richmond Park (Multi-Storey Apartment)

and reached approximately to 1280 families with appeal to source segregate.

2. It was observed that by routine monitoring and supervision by the project team total 323 families have started source segregation of waste at their home, which is 25.23 per cent of total covered population.
3. Referred to study by interns from TERI University, source segregation and project *Doh Bin* helped waste collectors to increase their income by 85 per cent and they could increase their income by learning to segregate more items from waste and by selling their waste items at higher rate.
4. It was observed that during the qualitative and quantitative survey of the waste generated in the project area the waste has better quality and more dry waste.
5. Project team was able to implement three bin systems in Richmond Park by putting separate bin for the collection of e-waste and prevent disposal of e-waste at landfill or processing through illegal channel.
6. Project team has started composting horticulture waste at Richmond Park and prevented huge quantity of horticulture waste reach to the landfill.
7. Waste collectors has started using gloves and mask during segregation that can protect them from many diseases skin and lung diseases.
8. Vertical Hydraulic Baler at Dry Waste Collection Centre has reduced work load on the workers and increased their work efficiency.
9. Waste contractor can store more waste material at the centre by compacting waste by the hydraulic baler, which may add more profit to their business.
10. Waste contractors are getting more value to the compact waste material because that reduced transportation cost at least 5 times.
11. Source segregation and increased recycling rate has also reduced the pressure on landfill site.
12. Project *Doh Bin* has brought stakeholders to a common platform to discuss their problem related to solid waste management. In this way a sustainable network build in the community.
13. Source segregation finds its place in people talks and action.

2.9 Conclusion

1. With the support from Coca-Cola India Pvt. Ltd. and Tetra Pak India Pvt. Ltd., RWA and other stakeholders IPCA successfully executed *Doh Bin* at DLF Phase-IV, Gurugram. 323 families joined the campaign by segregating waste at home and helped the waste collectors to earn more and live healthy life.
2. Solving the problem of waste management requires nothing less than a radical attitudinal change in the mindset of all stakeholders. This is best achieved through a co-operative effort which encourages a sense of stake holding in the entire process right from waste generation, primary collection, segregation, recycling, composting and final disposal. This involves a whole chain of people:
   - The generators (owners and household help) who need to be judicious;
   - The primary collectors (rag-picker) who need to be trained to reinforce segregation and recycling;
   - The disposers (corporation) who need to be conscientious in the final disposal process.

Case Study–III

We Care: India's First Joint EPR Initiative

WE CARE
Waste Efficient Collection and Recycling

3.1 Background

Globalization and industrialization have resulted in increased rate of generation for packaging waste in India. India generates 56 lakhs tonnes of plastic waste annually [Ministry of Environment, Forest and Climate Change (MoEF&CC), 2016a], out of which total plastic waste, which is collected and recycled in the country is estimated to be 9,205 tonnes per day (approximately 60% of total plastic waste), and 6,137 tonnes remain uncollected and littered. With an estimated packaging recycling rate of 30 per cent—India lags behind many other developed countries in recycling of these wastes. In India over the last few decades, the packaging industry in India has grown exponentially. If packaging materials are not disposed of correctly it ends up as a litter. In-order to cope with this problem, there is a need for developing a mechanism of segregation, collection and channelizing it to the right recycling industry for end of life solution and developing a sustainable supply chain of waste material. To develop sustainable supply chain and strengthen segregation and collection of plastic waste, lots of serious efforts need to be done at the ground with the collaboration of various stakeholders. Keeping this in mind, IPCA has been engaged by the Consortium to deal on the issue and demonstrate their commitment to implement effective plastic waste management system in India.

3.2 About the Consortium

A group of like-minded brand owner(s), recognizing the need to take the onus plastic waste took the Extended Producer Responsibility ("EPR"), as required under the provisions of the Plastic Waste Management Rules, 2016 ("Rules") (MoEF&CC, 2016b), to manage plastic waste generated by their respective companies. The Consortium comprises of representatives from the following companies:

I. PepsiCo India Holding Pvt. Ltd.
II. Nestle India Ltd.
III. Perfetti Van Melle India Private Ltd.
IV. Dharampal Satyapal Ltd.
V. Dabur India Ltd.

The Consortium proposed to undertake implementation of their EPR obligations, i.e. collection, segregation and recycling of the post-consumed Multi Layered Packaging (MLP) through Indian Pollution Control Association (IPCA), which has been working on similar initiatives in the past. This mission is across eight cities.

3.3 Objectives

- To educate waste pickers/waste dealers/traders/ aggregators on recycling properties of MLP and motivate them to collect and segregate it in the best possible way.
- To set up dry waste collection centre in metro cities with the help of local NGOs or waste management agencies to reduce the cost of logistics.
- To build up a network for collection and transportation of post-consumed MLP in metropolitan cities, in the first

phase, where the consumption of such a product is relatively high.

- To encourage people to participate in source segregation of waste for betterment of our environment.
- To explore new recyclers in different regions for maximum recycling of waste with higher margin of profit for waste pickers and lowest rate of logistics, eventually securing value for all stakeholders involved in this process of plastic waste management.

3.4 About the Supporting Partners

The action plan of the study was prepared under the expert guidance of Chairman, Central Pollution Control Board and subject expert Additional Director, Central Pollution Control Board. To fulfil the objectives of the project they got valuable support from different institutions and organizations, which helped them in different capacities. The leading supporting organization/institutes are as follow:

1. Central Pollution Control Board
2. East Delhi Municipal Corporation
3. East Delhi Waste Processing Company Ltd. (A Division of ILFS Environment)
4. ACC Ltd.
5. Ambuja Cement Ltd.
6. Geocycle Ltd.
7. Sampurn(e)arth Environment Solutions Pvt. Ltd., Mumbai
8. Eco Paryavaran Engineers & Consultants Pvt. Ltd., Chandigarh
9. Environment Matter, Chandigarh
10. PACE India, Uttrakhand
11. Bala Ji Enterprises, Mumbai

IPCA also met people from the following institutes and organization and got their best wishes for the successful implementation of project. They are hoping to get more support and we are in the process of signing agreement with these organizations:

1. Noida Authority,
2. Municipal Corporation Chandigarh,
3. Bombay Municipal Corporation.

3.5 Project Locations

The study was proposed in metro cities as the consumption of packaging waste material and waste generation rate is higher there. While the overall approach, in undertaking the EPR, in the long run, will remain "brand, category and geography neutral," following cities were identified for pilot phase of this project. They are:

I. Delhi
II. Noida (Dadri, Bulandshahar, Greater Noida)
III. Gurugram
IV. Ghaziabad (Muradnagar, Modinagar, Meerut)
V. Faridabad
VI. Chandigarh (Mohali, Ropar, Zirakpur, Panchkula)
VII. Mumbai
VIII. Dehradun (Haridwar, Rishikesh, Roorkee)

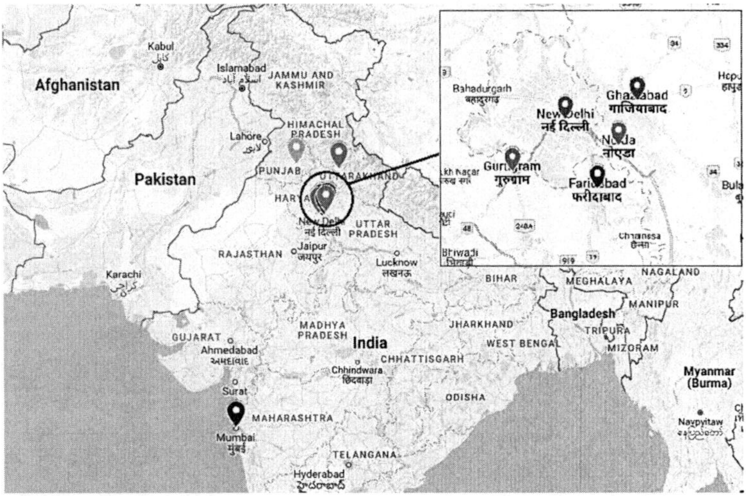

Figure 3.1: Selected areas for the study

3.6 Project Methodology

Following methodology was adopted to execute the action plan:

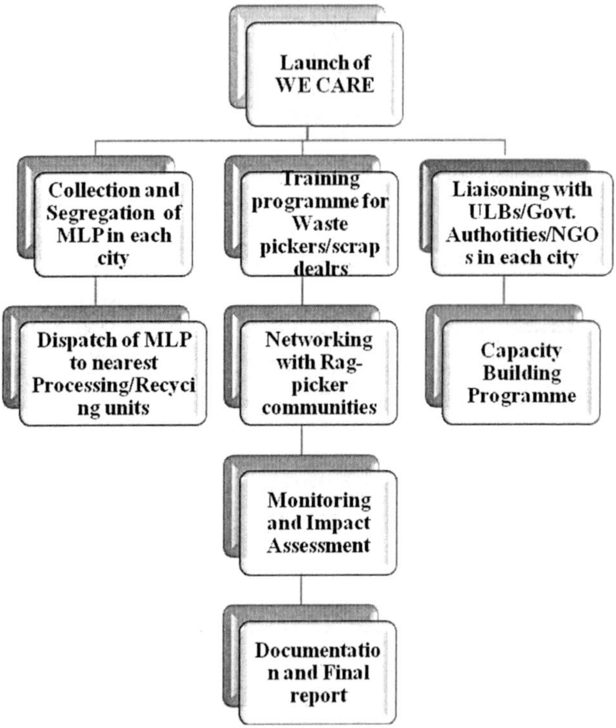

Figure 3.2: Steps of the Project

3.7 PROJECT ACTIVITIES

3.7.1 Launch of the "WE CARE"

The launch of India's first Joint EPR Initiative, "**WE CARE**" was held on 28th November, 2017 at Waste to Energy Plant of East Delhi Waste Processing Company Ltd. This project was supported by all stakeholders ranging from the brand owner, regulator, municipality, waste pickers and the processor, which make it more viable and sustainable. The launch was done in the presence of following dignitaries:

- Dr. Ranbir Singh (IAS), Commissioner, EDMC, Delhi
- Dr. S. K. Nigam, Additional Director, CPCB, Delhi
- Mr. Pradeep Khandelwal, Chief Engineer, EDMC
- Mr. Deepak Aggarawal, Senior Vice President, IL&FS Environment

And all five industries representatives:

- Mr. Samir Pathak, Director Corporate Affair, PepsiCo India Holding Put. Ltd.
- Mr. Barun Banerjee, Head Packaging, Nestle India Ltd.
- Mr. Atul Sud, Director Legal, Perfetti Van Melle
- Mr. Sameer Sharma Head-EHS, Dharampal Satyapal Ltd.
- Dr. Priyank Arya, Head-EHS, Dabur India Ltd.

Dr. Ranbir Singh said that every local authority is obliged under Plastic Waste Management (PWM) Rule 2016 to ensure scientific management and disposal of plastic waste. The project is pioneer initiative in the field of plastic waste management and will go long way. It will ensure Plastic free environment at the same time will improve the efficiency of waste to energy plant at Ghazipur and recycling of plastic waste along the value chain.

Dr. S. K. Nigam said that the collection, segregation, treatment and disposal of Multi-layered Packaging's (MLP) is a difficult path. Till now no institution or agency has achieved success in this area. CPCB in consultation with IPCA has initiated a project/pilot study with support of MLP consumers so called brand owners and EDMC. He wishes grand success of this innovative project.

All the consortium partners **showed their happiness towards this initiative and said that EPR is good for environment and nation and they are completely devoted to support EPR.**

A street play was then performed by IPCA team on MLP and the launch was ended with Logo revelation of "WE CARE" and Flag off to the loaded vehicle with post consumed MLP waste for processing at Waste to Energy Plant, Ghazipur, Delhi.

3.7.2 Networking with Waste Pickers Communities

Different clusters of waste pickers across the various cities in India and our team has worked hard to educate and aware them on MLP collection and segregation. Our team met with various waste pickers communities and educated them regarding the incentives of MLP collection and segregation. Through these training and workshops with rag-pickers communities, a network of approximate 1,500 waste pickers was developed in all project locations and they were continuously helping us in providing regular supply of post-consumed MLP waste for processing.

These waste pickers engaged in door-to-door collection of waste from households, markets, hotels, institutes etc. and recover recyclable material of their choice or which can be sold to the recyclers/scrap dealers/aggregators. Prior to WE CARE initiative, no waste picker was segregating MLP because there was no buyer and the entire MLP waste either dumped to landfill/roadside/river/drains/open space or burnt, which results in lots of environmental problems including air/water/land pollution.

Currently, approximately 1500 waste pickers are involved in collection and segregation of MLP waste and with their dedicated efforts toward the objective of WE CARE project, they collected 683.135 million ton (MT) of MLP waste.

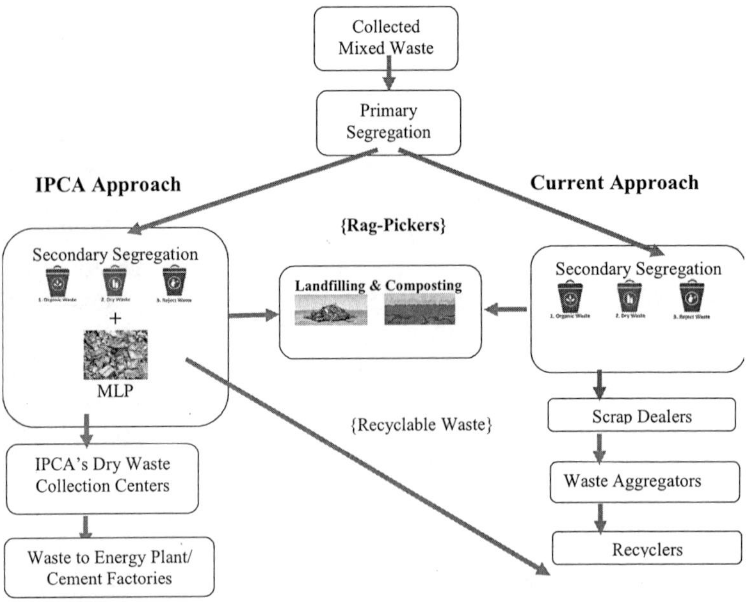

Figure 3.3: Collected Waste Treatment through current *v/s* IPCA approach

3.7.3 Education and Awareness Programme

In order to educate waste pickers/waste dealers/traders/aggregators about MLP and motivate them to collect and segregate, street plays and workshops were organized at different locations of the selected cities. IPCA is creating awareness among the waste pickers communities on the following points:

1. What is MLP?
2. Why is it important to collect and segregate MLP?
3. Why should we not littered or burnt MLP?
4. How are they get benefited for collection of MLP?
5. How can they contribute toward environment protection by collection and segregation of MLP?

Besides this they were also educated on their personal health and hygiene. In the first two months of project, IPCA has conducted 12 street plays and 6 workshops at the following locations on below mentioned dates. We got overwhelmed responses from the waste pickers after the street play and we are planning to do more street plays and workshops in coming days.

Table 3.1: Street Plays Details

Sl. No.	*Date*	*Locations*
		Delhi
1.	14-12-2017	Kanchan Kunj, Madanpur Khaddar
2.	14-12-2017	Samosa Chowk, Madanpur Khaddar
3.	18-12-2017	Pheri Basti, Shahbad Dairy
4.	18-12-2017	Shahbad Dairy, Daulatpur Kankarkhera Road
		Faridabad
5.	19-12-2017	Titu Colony
6.	19-12-2017	Dheeraj Nagar
		Gurugram
7.	27-12-2017	Mata Mandir Gali No 6, Near Global Hospital
8.	27-12-2017	Saraswati Kunj, Wazirabad
		Noida
9.	28-12-2017	Sarfabad, Sec-71,Noida
10.	28-12-2017	Barola, Sec-49, Noida
		Ghaziabad
11.	29-12-2017	Shalimar Garden
12.	29-12-2017	Bhopura

Table 3.2: Workshop Details

Sl. No.	*Date*	*Locations*
		Delhi
1.	05.01.2018	Khadar
2.	10.01.2018	Shahbad Dairy
		Noida
3.	24.01.2018	Sector-73, Sarfabad
		Gurugram
4.	25.01.2018	Nathupur
		Ghaziabad
5.	27.01.2018	Shalimar Garden
		Faridabad
6.	30.01.2018	Titu Colony

3.7.4 MLP Collection and Processing

A network of appx. 1,500 waste pickers in eight different cities, who were actively working in the field of collection and segregation of MLP. Collected 683.135 MT of MLP from all locations in a span of three months. The entire collected material was dispatched to East Delhi Waste Processing Company Ltd. at their Waste to Energy Plant, Ghazipur, Delhi, Geocycle Ltd. at their cement kiln plant at Gagal, Himachal Pradesh, and Deluxe Recycling Pvt. Ltd., Thane, Maharashtra.

The picture shows city-wise details of collection and dispatch of MLP have been provided in Table 3.2.

Figure 3.4: Collection and Dispatching of MLP

3.7.5 Liaisoning with Key Opinion Leaders (KOL)

Regular liaison with Key Opinion Leaders (KOL) of different organizations was instituted to seek their support in making WE CARE project more meaningful.

An agreement with EDMC, East Delhi Waste Processing Company Ltd., ACC Ltd. and Ambuja Cement Ltd., Geocycle Ltd., and Deluxe Recycling Pvt. Ltd for processing, co-processing and recycling of plastic waste were also signed.

3.8 Implementation Task Force

Following is the team engaged for executing the various activities in the all cities.

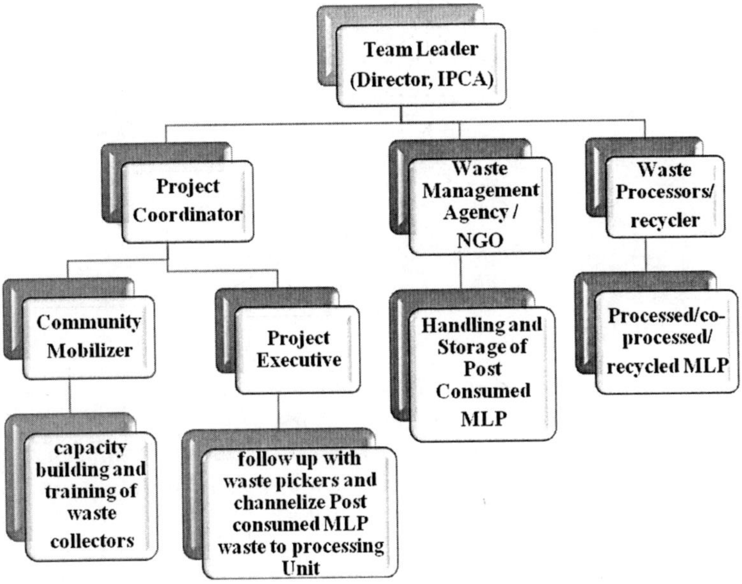

Figure 3.5: Team engaged for executing various activities in all the cities

3.9 Project Outcomes/Achievements

- Total MLP Collected: **683.115 MT**
- Total MLP Dispatched and Processed: **663.115 MT**

- Total Number of Waste collector/Segregator Involved: Approx. 1500

Table 3.3: MLP collection and dispatch Details

Sl. No.	*Cities/State*	*MLP Collected (MT)*	*MLP Dispatched / Processed (MT)*
1.	Delhi	235.80	235.80
2.	Noida (Dadri, Bulandshahar, Greater Noida)	30.060	30.060
3.	Ghaziabad (Muradnagar, Modinagar, Meerut)	191.408	191.408
4.	Gurugram	42.28	42.28
5.	Faridabad	62.172	62.172
6.	Chandigarh (Mohali, Ropar, Zirakpur, Panchkula)	28.480	13.40
7.	Mumbai	12.35	7.410
8.	Dehradun (Haridwar, Rishikesh)	43.395	43.395
9.	Jaipur	23.50	23.50
10.	Alwar	13.69	13.69
	Total	**683.135**	**663.115**

3.10 Challenges

The project is not without problems and challenges. Teams had many difficulties in executing the various project activities such as:

- Mobilizing and convincing various stakeholders for the collection and segregation of MLP.
- The rag pickers were not aware about this commodity so it was difficult to teach them but we used different modes to educate them like street plays and workshop.
- Our team is persistently involved in meeting and discussions with waste collectors, segregator, and scrape dealers to maximize the collection of MLP and govt. authorities and other organization to get support and consent for MLP collection.
- There were some issues with state authorities, who thought that there would be conflict of interest with the existing waste management agencies and these issues were resolved by subsequent discussions.

- There were some issues related to logistics, availability of KOL, communication from media etc. but we were able to resolved at our level best.

3.11 Impacts of "WE CARE"

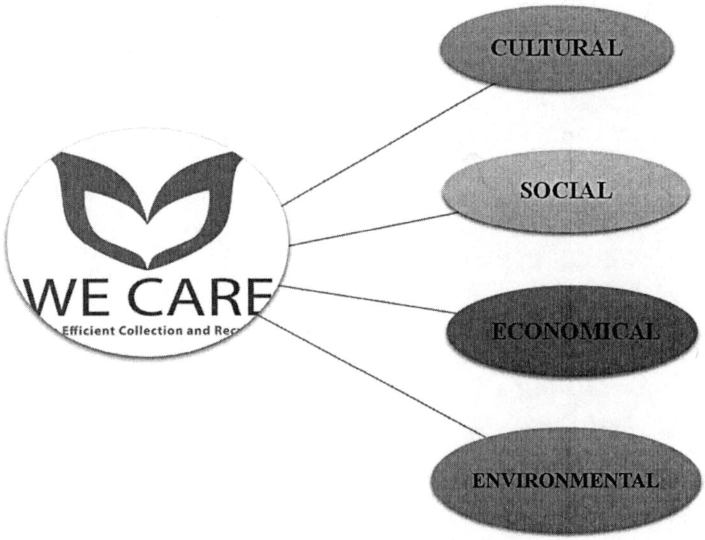

3.11.1 Cultural

Environment provides the resources to satisfy the basic needs of human life. Apart from this it plays an important role in the ethical, religious, social and cultural values of societies. Ecosystems provide many services to mankind such as recreation, tourism, etc. Benefits derived from the sustainable use of natural and environmental resources are generally categorized into three groups: ecosystem services, biological benefits and socio-economic benefits. Any degradation in ecosystems will not only affect production of plants and animals but also represent real threats to human life on the planet. Biological benefits represent the bulk of human consumption, whether direct consumptive use (i.e., food consumption, medicinal resources, wood products, breeding stocks etc.) or indirect consumptive use (i.e., recreation, bird watching, ecotourism etc.). Socio-economic benefits that can be generated from sustainable and efficient use of environmental resources include recreation and ecotourism. So, it is our cultural and moral responsibility to clean our mother earth and preserve it for our future generations.

3.11.2 Social

Waste pickers/waste dealers/traders/aggregators are educated through awareness camp, workshops and street plays on recycling properties of MLP and are motivated to collect and segregate it in best possible way. As most of the rag-picker communities were uneducated so street plays are used as the mode of education. The study involved people from various fields and communities, the interaction and communication has formed a linkage between them. To encourage people to participate in source segregation of waste for betterment of our environment, improving the environment and health condition of India through a recycling based waste management approach, WE CARE project is spreading awareness about health impacts and making society more responsible towards rag picker community and clean environment. These workshops will encourage people in source segregation. The project helps in changing the standard of living of rag-pickers.

3.11.3 Economical

The WE CARE projects help in optimum use of resources as the waste is segregated and processed in its best way.

The rag picker community is getting incentives for collection of MLP at the rate of **Rs. 7.00 per kg.** which is helping in raising the standard of their lives. Since approximately **1500 rag-picker** are involved in the collection and segregation of MLP in Eight Cities of India and on an average each rag-pickers has earned **Rs. 3190** in during this pilot project over his regular income. On the other hand in WE CARE project MLP is being used as an alternate source of energy in Waste to energy plant, cement production etc. as MLP has a high calorific value as compared to gasoline. Thus, it is indirectly helping in growth of Gross Domestic Product (GDP) of the country.

3.11.4 Environmental

India generates approximately 62 million tons of solid waste annually and maximum reach to the landfill site without treatment and processing, which is great threat to environment and also 9 per cent of total solid waste constitutes plastic waste, which comprises of different grades of plastic including MLP (MoEF&CC, 2016a).

If MLP would not have collected and processed, it would reach to either landfill or river bodies or parks or drain or burnt in uncontrolled environment, which may cause water/land/air pollution and poses health hazard to the people.

So, this project ultimately fighting with all types of pollution for the well-being of society and environment.

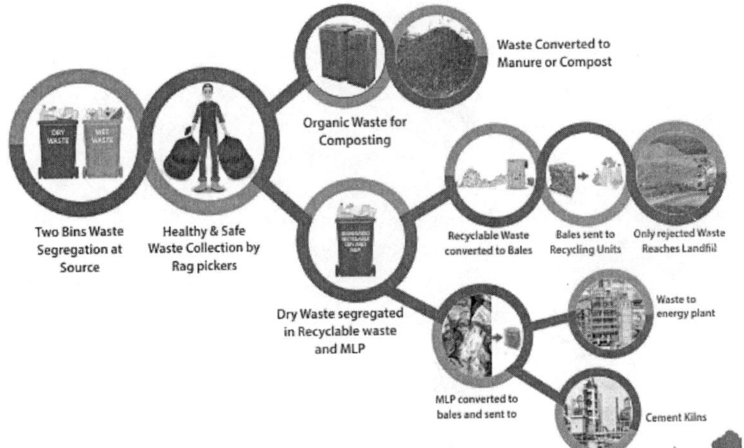

Figure 3.6: Supply Chain of Waste Management

3.12 Future Tasks and Targets

Future tasks concern increasing the network of all stakeholders across the India and collecting maximum amount of MLP, which will further result in safer environmental and better economic condition of rag-pickers communities. Our target is to collect maximum amount of MLP and to make maximum number of stakeholders educated and aware on MLP collection and segregation.

Case Study–IV

Campaign for Awareness about Pollution and its Remedial Measure

4.1 Background of the Project

Pollution prevention is a major global concern because of the harmful effects of pollution on a person's health and on the environment. Environmental pollution comes in various forms, such as: air pollution, water pollution, soil pollution, noise pollution etc. As can be witnessed, air quality in Indian cities is deteriorating day by day specially in Delhi NCR. Thirteen out of twenty most air polluted cities across the world are from India, and Delhi is on the top of it. As a result, number of hospital admissions and deaths are increasing due to air pollution exposure. As per the latest Lancet report, 2.5 million deaths in India are due to Air Pollution, which is the highest in the world. Similarly, water pollution has become a continuous increasing problem on the earth which is affecting the human and animal lives in all aspects. The whole water is getting polluted through many sources such as urban runoff, agricultural, industrial, sedimentary, leaching from landfills, animal wastes, and other human activities. In fact, it is said that almost 80 per cent of the water bodies in India are highly polluted. Ganga and Yamuna are the most polluted rivers in India.

All the types of pollution is very harmful to the environment. Human population is increasing day by day and thus their needs and competition is leading the pollution to the unstoppable levels. Everyone is a stakeholder as we are all inhabitants of this one and only mother earth. Each person can contribute something to advance environmental pollution mitigation measures. Environmental protection means caring for our resources and subsequently for ourselves and ensuring a sustainable future for generations to come will have a better environment.

Since, Quality Needles has been pioneer in spearheading environment-related activities as a part of their Corporate Social Responsibility; "**Campaign for Pollution and its Remedial Measures**" Project is one of its initiatives to create awareness related to environmental pollution and its remedial measures among the school children. Since, today's children are tomorrow's leaders. As role **models**, parents and educators it is the need to teach the children how to care about the environment. If there was no water there would be no life on earth, air is the resource for which the supply is seemingly endless but these are often taken for granted and abused through human actions. A great deal of the pollution stems from our everyday activities, and there are several basic lifestyle changes we can make to protect this precious resource. Through education and awareness, we can lead children into a brighter, cleaner future. Thus, this project envisages motivating and training about five hundred students of ten schools in Delhi NCR through conducting workshops to sensitize the children on environmental pollution, types, issues, their causes and concerns, how to reduce their personal exposure. Special emphasis will be given on to reduce various pollution levels and protect the environment through various actions at different levels of society.

4.2 About the Project

The campaign is designed for children aged 13-16 years, which imparted training in a workshop spread over two days. The details of schools contacted is attached in section 4.10 as Annexure-II. The awareness and training will be imparted through interactions and practical demonstrations during workshops to a group of fifty students and each participant will be christened as 'Environment Managers' and would be provided with badges accordingly.

4.3 Project Objectives

The proposed project aims to train and sensitize five hundred school children from ten Schools on various aspect of environmental pollution including identification of different kind of pollution and its source, monitoring of pollutants, different approach to reduce its impact on individuals. The key objectivss:e of the campaign is to motivate students to come up with their own ideas to improve and conserve environment and implement their ideas in the form of doable actions.

A number of ways, were adopted to achieve the above objectives and meet the challenges, are:

(a) Interactions, distribution of printed material and audio-visual presentations.
(b) Screening of educative short films on environment pollution.
(c) Games for students and teachers related to Environment Management activities.
(d) Quiz, poster and slogan competition for the students.
(e) Field visits to sites to show them real life causes and solutions of pollution.

4.4 Methodology

The project was executed in ten different schools of Delhi/NCR and was carried out in two phases, in first phase, a workshop was organized in schools and in second phase a field visit was organized for students. Following is the methodology we adopted for the project:

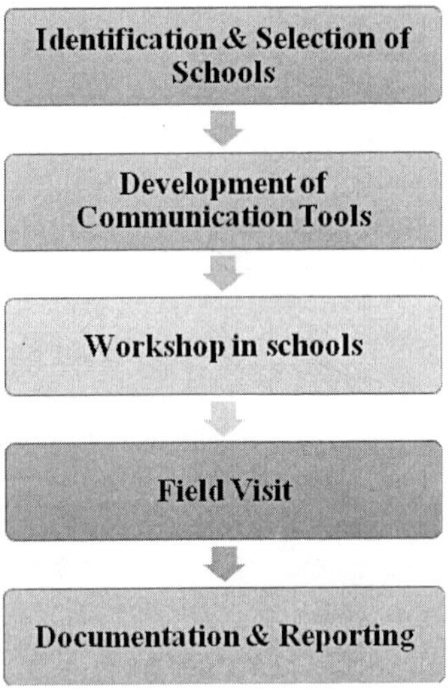

Figure 4.1: Steps of the Project

4.5 Project Activities

4.5.1 *Identification and Selection of Schools*

Following schools were selected in Delhi/NCR under the project:

Table 4.1: List of Selected Schools

Sl. No.	*Location*
1.	Amar Public School, Sector-37, Noida
2.	Vivekanand International School
3.	Lord Mahavira Model School Sector-29, Noida
4.	Laxmi Public School
5.	Model National School Sector-45 Noida
6.	Marrigold Public School Sector-19, Noida
7.	Marrigold Public School Greator Noida
8.	Yash Memorial School
9.	Sapphire International School
10.	Arunodaya Public School

4.5.2 *Development of Communications Tools*

The project team developed various communications tools to train and educate school students to meet the above mentioned objectives which are as follows:

- Audio-visual presentations on pollution, its type, causes, impacts and mitigation measures.
- Short animated movie and educational movie to motivate the students on various aspects of pollution.
- Handbook on Nature Conservation through Pollution Control.
- Illustrations, Posters, Charts, and display board on guidelines of pollution control.
- Badges for students with project name and a message **"I care for my Environment"**.
- Fun learning games related to pollution.
- Multiple Choice quizzes to evaluate the knowledge and understanding of students.

4.5.3 Workshop in Schools (Phase-I)

The first phase of the project was the introductory phase for the students and they were made aware about the objectives of the project, people and organization involved in execution of the project followed by audio-video presentation on environment pollution. In each session more than 50 students were present mostly from classes VII-IX. The sessions were made very interactive by conducting some fun loving activities and students were encouraged and motivated to ask questions and share their views. Short animated video and other informative short videos were showcased during phase I to enhance student's knowledge through different modes of communication and generate interest in the subject.

Students were also asked to take assignments on environment pollution in the form of poster making or slogan and poem writing. A handbook on **"Nature Conservation through Pollution Control"**, pamphlets and badges were distributed to each student of the project and illustrative chart on pollution and its guideline were handed over to school administration during the first visit of Phase-I. At the end of the overall session children pledged to keep the environment clean.

4.5.4 Field Visit (Phase-II)

Field Trip was organized at Eco and Environment Park, Sector 54, Noida to demonstrate the solar panel, vermi-composting site, herbal, rainwater harvesting model. A quiz competition was conducted in which students were asked to solve multiple questions answers. Prizes and certificates were given to winners of the posters making, slogans writing and quiz competition. Consolation certificates were given to all the students who participated in the activities.

4.6 Milestones Achieved

The following milestones have been achieved under this project:

- The project has been executed in all the schools in two phases as per the proposed timeline.
- The programme has helped to arouse the interest of the school students towards the environment and its protection.
- Trained students have learnt all aspects of all kind of pollution, issues related to them and their remedial measures.
- These trained students have been empowered to help schools in implementing improvement measures

whenever required like monitoring school cleanliness, placement of adequate number and kind of dustbins in optimum positions to eliminate littering, stop burning of all kinds of waste, maximum use of public transport, use of bicycles etc.

4.7 Challenges

It was quite difficult to coordinate with school and get dates for workshop and other activities as schools were pre-occupied with exams or some other activities.

4.8 Impact of the Project

The impact of this programme is such that students have become more responsible towards environment and they had become more pro-active towards issues of various Environment Pollutions, which has been reflected from the slogan, posters and poems made by them.

The project has helped to inculcate the basic practices in their daily routine which can help in conserving the environment and reducing the environment pollution such as planting more and more trees, using bicycle for school, avoiding private transport instead using public one, using two dustbins (Blue and Green) for throwing waste etc. As a result of this project students who are citizens of tomorrow were motivated towards creating a sustainable environment.

4.9 Feedback from the School Management

The feedback for the school management regarding the project activities so as to assess the success of the project and also to improve upon the activities if any suggested by them was executed. As per their feedback the activities proposed in the project were well designed and executed in a well-planned manner. The project has benefited more than five hundred students from ten different schools from Delhi/NCR region. In all the schools the two phased programme was very much appreciated by the students as well as the teachers, who felt that the programme helped in understanding the problem of environment pollution amongst the children and the participating schools.

The classroom session as well the field visits were very informative and interactive for the students and gave equal opportunity to share their views and interact with the experts. It helped to clear many concepts and misconceptions of the students. Through simple activities students were told about the environment pollution and its remedial measures and simple habits that one should inculcate in order to combat the problem of environment pollution. Children enjoyed the classroom sessions and the activities conducted. The field visit enhanced their knowledge about environment and do's and don'ts about it since it was practically demonstrated to them.

ANNEXURE-II

List of Schools Contacted

Sl. No.	Location	Principal Name	Contact No.	Contact Person	Contact No.	Email	First visit	Second Visit
1.	Amar Public School, Sector-37, Noida	Ms. Raj Bhandari	9899874777	Ms. Hemlata Chobey	9891320907		15/12/2017	16/04/2018
2.	Vivekanand International School	Sonu Kundra	9868001576	Ms. Nirmala	7042628813	vivekanandinternational school@yahoo.in	20/12/2017	
3.	Lord Mahavira Model School Sector-29, Noida	Mr. P.K. Jain	9810983650	Mr. Bala	9540279646	lord.mahavira@yahoo.in	22/12/2017	02/04/2018
4.	Laxmi Public School	Ms. Anita Vashit	011-22376937	Mr. D.D Sharma	9811852656	laxmipublicschool@gmail.com	19/01/2018	25/04/2018
5.	Model National School Sector-45,Noida	Mr. Dharmender Sharma	8800832489	Mr. Harvinder	9958002993	dharmender1980@gmail.com	22/01/2018	26/04/2018
6.	Marrigold Public School Sector-19, Noida	Mr. V.K. Sharma	9811703320	Ms. Gargi	9811215554	marrigoldpublicschool@gmail.com	23/01/2018	18/04/2018
7.	Marrigold Public School Greator Noida	Mr. Mohit Sharda	9811126492	Ms Parveen Goel	9871040355	principal@mpsgnoida.com	29/01/2018	01/05/2018
8.	Yash Memorial School	MS. R. Mukherjee	8750069281			yashmemorialschool@yahoo.com	2/2/2018	24/04/2018
9.	Arunodaya Public School	Mrs. Sangeeta Naga	011-22371019	Ms. Kakoli	9911727402	arunodayaschool@rediffmail.com	12/4/2018	11/05/2018
10.	Sapphire International School			Mr. Ajay Mishra	8130350881			19/04/2018

Bibliography

Adams, Anne and Cox, Anna L. (2008). "Questionnaires, in-depth interviews and focus groups", In: Cairns, Paul and Cox, Anna L. eds. (*Research Methods for Human Computer Interaction*, Cambridge, UK: Cambridge University Press, pp. 17–34.) Retrieved from *http://oro.open.ac.uk/11909/1/9780521870122c02_p17-34.pdf*

Mishra, L. (2016). "Focus group discussion in qualitative research", *TechnoLEARN*, Vol. 6, No. 1, pp. 1-5, June 2, Retrieved from *https://ndpublisher.in/admin/issues/tlV6N1a.pdf*

MoEF&CC (2016a). *Solid Waste Management Rules Revised After 16 Years: Rules Now Extend to Urban and Industrial Areas.* Retrieved from *http://pib.nic.in/newsite/PrintRelease.aspx?relid=138591*

MoEF&CC (2016b). *Government Notifies Plastic Waste Management Rules, 2016.* Retrieved from *http://pib.nic.in/newsite/printrelease.aspx?relid=138144*

Monde (2016). *The KAP Survey Model (Knowledge, Attitudes, and Practices).* Retrieved from *https://www.spring-nutrition.org/publications/tool-summaries/kap-survey-model-knowledge-attitudes-and-practices*

Ross, Kenneth N. (2005). *Quantitative Research Methods in Educational Planning,* Retrieved from *http://unesdoc.unesco.org/images/0021/002145/214555E.pdf*

The Lancet (2017). *The Lancet Commission on Pollution and Health.* Retrieved from *https://www.thelancet.com/journals/lancet/article/PIIS0140-6736(17)32345-0/fulltext#main-menu*

Zia, Hina; Devadas, V. and Shukla, S. (2008). "Assessing informal waste recycling in Kanpur City, India", *Management of Environmental Quality: An International Journal,* 19(5):597-612, Retrieved from *https://www.researchgate.net/publication/242021324_Assessing_ informal_waste_recycling_in_Kanpur_City_India*

Index